T0095412

FOLLOWSHIP

Bryan W. Horne

FOLLOWSHIP 101

All scriptures are cited from the King James Version & New Living
Translation of the Bible unless paraphrased for context and clarification.
iUniverse books may be ordered through booksellers or by contacting:

iUniverse
1663 Liberty Drive
Bloomington, IN 47403
www.iuniverse.com
1-800-Authors (1-800-288-4677)

ISBN: 978-1-4917-6587-6 (sc)
ISBN: 978-1-4917-6586-9 (e)

Library of Congress Control Number: 2015906021

Print information available on the last page.

iUniverse rev. date: 04/28/2015

Contents

Dedication

Followship 101 is dedicated to my Redeemer, Jesus Christ. He is my example for everything. I am so grateful to the Lord for being my all in all. My heart's desire is to follow Him all the days of my life. Thank You for the incredible men You have given me the honor and privilege of serving these twenty years of ministry: J. D. Bowen, Matt Kunkel, Wayne Swanson, and my Pastor, Hart Ramsey. I am who I am as a result of the influence of the Holy Spirit and the connection to the men I have served.

I would like to honor my Pastor and mentor of more than fourteen years. Your deposit in my life has created a vessel that is profitable for the ministry. My connection to you is my life's greatest honor. Serving you and the amazing NCC vision is my passion and purpose. Thank you for believing in me when others would not. Thank you for believing in me and seeing ministry left in me when others could not. Everything I know of any value—you have taught me. The journey has been amazing, and we are looking forward to grace-filled days ahead.

I would like to thank my wife and best friend, Shannon, for being a helpmate who allows me to serve with my whole heart. My assignment is impossible without your heart and sacrificial service to me, our girls, and our lives' purpose.

Your faithfulness and commitment to me and the assignments we have been given are unmatched in the earth. Serving with you is my greatest joy in life. You were the first and only person I gave my heart to. Proverbs 18:22 says, a man who finds a wife finds a "good thing" and obtains favor from the Lord. I am that man, and the favor of the Lord is ours. I love you!

To my beautiful princesses, Jordan Marie and Logan Grace, thank you for following my lead and trusting me to be your mentor and biggest fan. Your destinies are upon you both, and the favor upon your lives is undeniable. Stay grateful, serve with your whole heart, and be the leaders you were made to be. Dad loves you! #TeamHorne

A special thank you to my NCC Dothan, Safe Harbor, and ATL South Family: your love and support of me and my family over the years is unexplainable. I am eternally grateful for the opportunity and privilege to be in your midst. I love you!

#WeAreThatChurch

Foreword

If there's anyone in the world qualified to write about following, it is Pastor Bryan Horne. *Followship* is an art. It's a gift from God, given to those humble enough to understand that anything can be accomplished when ego takes a backseat to vision. In this book, you will discover a higher level of thinking and a deeper level of living. The singular command of Jesus to His disciples was "Follow me." But not everyone gets what it really means to follow.

So read this book with an open mind. And by the final chapter, you just may find your higher purpose in life. You just may find the fulfillment you've been searching for your entire life. May God use this book to give your life purpose. May God use these words to make us all first-class followers of Jesus Christ.

This book is going to bless the world!

Pastor Hart Ramsey
Founder and Senior Pastor
Northview Christian Church

Confirmation

*... the Lord said to David, I took you from
the sheepfold, from following the sheep, to
be ruler over my people, over Israel.*
—2 Samuel 7:8

The greatest leaders are those who first followed well. Even Jesus was not intimidated by being called a servant.

I can think of no better place for a person to start toward leadership than to first learn to be a follower, and I can think of no better book or person to begin that journey with than this book and Bryan Horne.

Loyal, laboring, loving, and continually learning—these are the words and works that speak of Bryan. Bryan teaches only that which has been "wrought" in him first (Romans 15:18).

Don't just read this book; let this book read you. If you do, your life will bear the same fruit and favor of its writer.

Pastor Phil Munsey
Chairman of the Champion Network of Pastors,
Joel Osteen Ministries
Lakewood Church, Houston, Texas

Affirmation

This is a book so filled with honor. It honors the established leadership of your local church, which invariably builds the heart of your leader. In a cynical time in the earth, we need a book that is rooted in honor.

Secondly, the clear, applicable, and easy-to-understand principles are not so far above the average reader that he or she can't grab them and make them his or her own. Bryan has a writing style that invites people in and doesn't "write down" to them.

Sometimes people with great expertise write in order to impress themselves. This is not the case with you. It is clear from your content what your heart's intent is: to encourage and empower people to understand the power of *Followship*, which leads to greater places of intimacy and fellowship.

Congratulations, my friend! Love you!

John Gray
Associate Pastor
Lakewood Church
Houston, Texas

Special Thanks

Pastor Hart Ramsey
Founder and Senior Pastor of Northview Christian
Church—Dothan and Montgomery, Alabama, and
ATL, Georgia
www.nccfamily.org

Pastor Phil Munsey—Houston, Texas
Chairman of Champions Network
Joel Osteen Ministries

Pastor John Gray—Houston, Texas
Associate Pastor at Lakewood Church

Michael Carson—Montgomery, Alabama
Owner of MCarson Photography
www.mcarsonphotography.com

Marcus T. Crawford—Montgomery, Alabama
CEO/Owner of MC2O Design
www.mc2odesign.com

Introduction

Then he said to the crowd, "If any of
you wants to be my follower, you must
turn from your selfish ways, take up
your cross daily, and follow me."
Luke 9:23 NLT

Where would we be if we studied *Followship* before
we studied leadership? We live in a society where
leadership is applauded and celebrated, while
following is seldom discussed but often demanded
by those who are usually self-appointed to lead.
Everybody wants to lead, but very few have ever
mastered the art of following.

Before our journey takes flight, it is critical to
note that I have not personally mastered the art of
following. However, the answer to the question as
to what makes me uniquely qualified to write this
book is rooted in thirty years of following Christ
and over twenty years of ministry. The experiences
and opportunities in ministry to follow great men
throughout my life have given me very insightful
and revelatory wisdom on the art of following.
I have had the privilege of serving some of the
greatest men in the body of Christ, the greatest of
whom I have been honored to serve for the past
fourteen years in the massive vision of Pastor

Hart Ramsey and Northview Christian Church. It is my prayer that through the grace of our Lord Jesus Christ and the power of the precious Holy Spirit this book will unlock truths of the favor and abundant blessing that comes from following Christ and those He has appointed you to serve.

The reality is, if no one is following you, you are not really leading. There has to be someone following you for you to call yourself a true leader. As a matter of fact, only those who are following you are qualified to call you a leader. You cannot call yourself a leader. Many in the church desperately want to lead, but the truth is most cannot get their own family to follow them, much less others.

True leadership is only birthed through the lessons and experiences gained by laying your life down for another. The degree to which you are willing to be abased and follow is the degree to which the Lord is able to promote and exalt you in due season. The Lord has no shortage of abundance, favor, and resources for those who imitate His example of following. To truly be like Christ, we must receive and apply this practical example of the ministry of the Lord Jesus Christ.

Where would the body of Christ be if the twelve disciples never made the decision to be followers of Jesus? I argue that we would have never heard the gospel of Jesus Christ! Jesus called the disciples to be His followers, not His leaders. The disciples walked out a three-year journey to learn how to become followers, not leaders. They were then launched into the role of leadership as a result of their ability to grow through the process of following. In Luke 9:23, *followship* is described as consisting of a three-step process that is developed over time. It doesn't happen automatically overnight.

The Followship Process

1. Turn from your selfish ways.
2. Take up your cross.
3. Follow Jesus.

During our journey together, we will embark upon the definition of *followship*, with Jesus as the perfect example; the three-step process of followship; and the benefits that are released upon those who follow. Take a few moments now and ask the Holy Spirit to open your heart and mind to receive everything He has for you. Let's begin our journey together on the road called Followship 101 and learn how to be all the Lord has called us to be. My prayer is that the abundant life of Christ be revealed to you along this journey, as we continue to look to Jesus as the author and finisher of our faith and grow in the grace and knowledge of our Lord and Savior Jesus Christ.

Chapter 1

Followship Defined

If learning to lead is called leadership, then learning to follow must be called *followship*. Before anything can be explained, it must first be defined. I do need a little creative liberty and license to use the English language to create a term we are not so familiar with. I must explain that my first language is English and I do understand that the word *followship* is not in Webster's Dictionary. However, the word *follow* is. According to Merriam-Webster's, the word *follow* is a Middle English verb that means to go, proceed, or come after. Another definition is to engage in, as in a calling or a way of life. The suffix "ship" indicates something that shows or possesses a quality, state, or condition. Each of these definitions are critical to our understanding of *followship*.

The first thing we discover is that the word

follow is a verb. This is important because following is an action. However, the action is first mental and even emotional before the physical act of following takes place. Following is seldom sincere and pure if the motivation to follow is rooted in manipulation, coercion, domination, or pressure. You must have a personal revelation and willingness to respond to the choosing of the Lord to submit to whom and where you are being called to follow. There must be a unity between the spirit, soul, and the body for true following to take place. Most of what we do in life profits little if the attitude and intention of our heart is not right before the Lord. The Lord alone knows every desire and intention of our heart toward everything we pursue and attempt.

Whatever you go after in life is an indicator of who you are actually following. Some people pursue wealth, while others spend their lives going after power, fame, and status. Whom or what you come after will determine the destination your future will reach. Following is always directional and geographical. The person you are called to follow and where the person is going is critical to your purpose and destiny. Just because you call yourself a leader doesn't mean you are a leader. If you call yourself a leader and no one is following you, you are actually just taking a walk!

Followship is a calling in life. It is equated to an engagement. The power of an engagement describes the commitment involved in following someone in a mutual agreement for a specified amount of time until a permanent agreement is made publicly. Many times, people will launch out into a public ministry without taking the appropriate time to walk out the private engagement season where true development occurs. Moses prepared eighty years before walking in his purpose. One of the qualifications for the high priest in Israel was that he be at least thirty years old. Even Jesus prepared thirty years for three and a half years of ministry and purpose.

Jesus knew the price of following more than any other person in the universe. He had fully counted the cost of following His Father unto complete perfection. The commitment Jesus made to leave heaven and come to earth on behalf of the Father was the greatest sacrifice ever made. Therefore, before He asked His disciples to follow Him, the word *follow* had great meaning to the one true Son of the living God.

There are two primary forms of authority in the earth:

1. Divine authority
2. Delegated authority

The Roman centurion found in Matthew 8 and Luke 7 gives us the perfect example of how divine and delegated authorities operate in the earth. The centurion soldier knew by revelation and experience that true authority comes from whom you follow, not whom you lead. His response to Jesus was, "I am a man in authority because I am a man under authority, so I can tell one to go and they will go and tell another to come and they will come." His revelation created faith to tell Jesus, "You don't even have to come to my house and pray for my servant, just speak the Word and my servant will be whole." Jesus marveled at this Gentile's faith and told him He had not seen faith like his in all of Israel.

Divine authority comes directly from the Lord Himself. God has given authority to mankind in a variety of different ways. Since creation, man has walked in divine authority and dominion over the animal kingdom, the land, and the sea. As believers, we have divine authority because of the finished work of Jesus Christ. Because of the death, burial, and resurrection of Jesus, we have been given divine authority straight from Him; we are seated together with Him in heavenly places, according to the book of Ephesians.

The greatest form of divine authority we have been given as believers under the administration of Grace is our tongue. We have been given the power to create death and life by the words we speak, according to Proverbs 18:21. The word *power* denotes a hand that creates and produces. Every tongue has a hand that creates or destroys by simply speaking. Abraham, by faith, was able to speak to those things that were not as though they were. The book of Hebrews chapter 1 describes how the worlds were framed by the Word of God. This innate divine power has been given to us as heirs of God and joint heirs with Christ Jesus.

The words we speak carry much greater weight and value in our daily lives than we give them credit for. Our words, in actuality, build roads into our future, creating the destiny in which we will walk. The words we speak today will guarantee the future we experience tomorrow. The Lord's promise for the believer is to make crooked paths straight. This can only be done as we use our divine authority and say what He says about our lives. If words can create worlds, then how much impact can our words have on the details of our daily lives? Our words alone do not carry great weight, but the Word of God carries unlimited, exponential weight in the earth as it does in heaven. That is why it is critical to know what God has already said about you, your past, your present, and your future—you can say what He has said until you see what He sees for you. Guard your heart, for the Bible says that out of the heart flow the issues of life (our words).

Divine authority and the words we speak are critical to our growth into *followship*. What we say about ourselves and those we follow will greatly affect our course and assignment. Confession is made as a result of our believing. What you believe is important, because what you believe you will always speak, intentionally or unintentionally. For out of the abundance of the heart, the mouth always speaks. The heart leaks life through the words of our mouth, springing from the meditation of our hearts.

Delegated authority is given from one person to another and always carries responsibility. You cannot have authority without responsibility. Responsibility with no authority is not authority at all and is crippling to every assignment in the earth. God in His divine creation would never have left us in the earth with responsibility and no authority in which to operate.

All power and authority ultimately comes from God Himself. However, to fulfill purpose and destiny, God allows people to delegate authority to others to increase the impact and effectiveness of the assignment at hand. Jesus told His disciples that they would do greater things than He did because of the power of delegated authority. He was limited in an earthly body, but His Spirit in them would make them limitless and more effective than ever before to reach the entire world with the Good News of the gospel of Jesus.

We see delegated authority in every area of our lives. In politics, entertainment, civil matters, the judiciary, society, business, and especially our military, you can see the direct effects of delegated authority. Why are we so shocked when we see delegated authority in the kingdom of God in our local churches? Our God is a God of order, and He does everything decently and in order. We appreciate order when we see its benefit but oftentimes reject it when it is required of us for the benefit of the whole. Order is God's plan to simplify our lives. Everything has a place and a responsibility, which creates an atmosphere of order and peace. *Followship* requires the understanding of order to receive the full benefit of working as a team for the benefit of the whole and not just an individual.

Finally, we must establish what the Gospel is before we launch into our journey of learning true *followship*. The Gospel is the foundation of any true leadership and *followship* relationship in the earth. First, the Gospel is not a what but rather a *who*. The Gospel is the person of Jesus Christ. It's not the gospel "of" Jesus; Jesus is actually the personification of the Gospel. Jesus is the Gospel. The Bible explains in the Gospel of John that "For the Law was given **by** Moses, but Grace and Truth came **by** Jesus Christ" (John 1:17 KJV).

The Gospel is also referred to as Good News and ultimately revealed as Grace to all believers after Jesus' ascension and glorification back to the right hand of our Father in heaven. The Grace of God is not an upgraded administration of the Law but a completely new administration with new rules, benefits, promises, and provisions. Every benefit, promise, and provision under the Grace administration is far better than the administration under the law.

In a nutshell, *Grace* is defined as the revelation and acceptance by faith that Jesus has done everything for us, as opposed to under the Law where we try endlessly to do everything ourselves, only to fail miserably and repeatedly. Why would we continue to do for ourselves what Jesus has already done for us? For example, because of the death, burial, and resurrection of Christ, the Bible repeatedly declares, we have been made right with God. So why would we continue to attempt things in our own effort and strength to attain a right standing with God when we are already right with God by believing in what Jesus has already done for us? The answer is found in knowing that religion is humanity's attempt to get to God in our own efforts, while relationship is God's way of doing the work for us and inviting us into fellowship with Him through faith in Christ alone.

Everyone in relational roles of leadership and *followship* in the earth must understand the power of Grace (Jesus) to truly succeed. As you read throughout the Bible, it is safe to insert the name Jesus every time you see the word *Grace*. Under the Law, all the demands and responsibility were placed on humankind. Under Grace, the demand was satisfied through the finished work of Jesus for those who believe. The Grace of God is Jesus, and without Him, we can do nothing! Our lives cannot succeed by our own might or power, but must be fully accomplished by the power of the Spirit of Jesus. On Calvary, Jesus declared, "It is finished"! Death, hell, and the grave lost their grip for eternity the moment Jesus sat up and walked out of the borrowed tomb three days and three nights later with the keys and all power in His hand.

The Grace of God is the operative power of God. Grace (Jesus) is the Father's ultimate divine action toward all humankind.

Grace has many sides and manifestations, so we must access and receive every available Grace that Jesus offers for our daily lives. His Grace is unlimited, so continue to ask for all you need as you walk in faith, resting in what Jesus has done for you.

Let's prepare our hearts now to see these three practical steps to *followship* and unlock our ability to walk out our divine destiny in the earth as followers.

Prayer

Lord Jesus, open my eyes that I may see You!

Notes

Chapter 2

Turn from Your Selfish Ways

Then he said to the crowd, "If any of
you wants to be my follower, you must
turn from your selfish ways, take
up your cross daily, and follow me."
Luke 9:23 NLT

The first step Jesus addresses in becoming a
follower is to deal with the natural inclination
that all of humanity has toward selfishness. You
cannot follow and be selfish at the same time. It is
impossible! *Followship* immediately attacks and
reveals the innate desire in us to think of ourselves
first. The reason most of us do not follow well is
because of the inability to not make ourselves the
center of our own universe.

Almost every decision we make on a daily basis

is centered on how the outcome will affect us. Then, we measure the effect on those around us from the closest of friends to those whom we fellowship with on an acquaintance level. Before ever considering to whom or where our *followship* may lead us, we must first address self. Following requires a denial of self for the benefit and betterment of those we are following or serving.

Putting others first is a challenge in friendship, marriage, and even business. True friendships are rooted in selfless acts of kindness and concern through life's most difficult seasons and challenges. It's impossible to be a great friend and be selfish at the same time. Nobody wants to be a friend to a selfish person who always thinks of him or herself first. Many marriages fail because of selfishness in the relationship. You can't always have it your way and expect to have a healthy relationship that is mutually rewarding. Many people in marriage would rather be right than have peace, which leads to constant nagging, bickering, and fighting.

The apostle Paul in the book of Ephesians clearly explains that the husband must love his wife as Christ loves the Church and gave Himself for her. The husband is to nurture her, take care of her, and love her as he does himself. The Lord is not saying don't take care of yourself, but He is saying you should do the same for your spouse.

In business, if your bottom line is the primary motivation and focus, then you will not succeed.

The majority of businesses are birthed out of a vision that answers a need to help solve a problem or simplify people's lives. Businesses that succeed are usually redemptive in their inception, which means they help deliver or rescue people from a predicament. It can be natural or spiritual and as simple as helping people with their time management skills or as complex as helping people with their very own souls.

Selfishness is the greatest enemy of unity. Satan uses selfishness as the fuel to divide families, churches, businesses, and every type of relationship in the earth. Since the beginning, Satan has used selfishness to destroy relationships. All three areas of temptation attack our innate selfish desire to satisfy our own needs and wants above anyone or anything. The only three strategies the enemy has at his disposal to attack us are the same three he has used since the beginning. It was in the garden planted eastward in Eden where Adam and Eve found themselves dealing with an enemy called Satan, cloaked in the form of a serpent. The three areas of temptation for all humanity are described in 1 John 2:16:

1. Lust of the flesh
2. Lust of the eyes
3. The pride of life

Selflessness is the denial of your rights, roles,

and responsibilities for the vision of another. This is the greatest challenge of *followship*. You must deal with self first in order to follow with sincerity and purity of heart. In a time where everyone wants to protest and demand his or her rights, the body of Christ is facing its greatest shortage of followers in the history of the church. The promoting, marketing, and branding of self is at an all-time high in the world.

Where are the ministries of helps and service in the kingdom? These ministries require a denying of self and promoting of the one who has sent you! Remember: His ways are higher than our ways and His thoughts are higher than our thoughts. As far as the heavens are above the earth, so are the ways of the Lord. The Lord always sees the end from the beginning, so His vantage point is His advantage and is crucial to His plan. That is why He encourages us throughout His Word to "Trust in the Lord with all thine heart; and lean not unto thine own understanding. In all thy ways acknowledge Him, and He shall direct thy paths." (Proverbs 3:5-6 KJV)

From the cradle to the grave, our lives must be centered on following the leading of the Lord. In Psalm 23, David reveals the Lord as our Shepherd, who leads us in the paths of righteousness for His namesake. He will always lead you in the right way because His way is the right way. The way may not always look right or even feel right, but trust becomes the greatest resource we possess in our personal relationship with the Lord.

Nobody promotes like the Lord. Jesus is the ultimate divine promoter because true promotion always comes from Him and Him alone. The Lord's promotion is a blessing from Him that makes one rich and adds no sorrow with it. Being rich is not just having financial success but touches every area of your life. Wholeness is the ultimate goal for every believer. Money without health is of no benefit, while health with no money is depressing. Wholeness benefits us spiritually, physically, mentally, emotionally, relationally, and financially.

It is impossible to have your way and the Lord's way at the same time. We must first acknowledge that the Lord's way is best. His way is always for our good and for His glory. Once you submit your will to His will, your will and His will synchronize to become one. Now, you will begin to walk in such intimacy with the Lord that He will give you even the desires of your heart, because your heart and His heart have become one.

The Lord will first deal with your "want to," because our selfishness is expressed through our desires. Many of our desires are inward, but once they sit long enough in the recesses of our hearts, they eventually come forth through the words of our mouths. Out of the abundance of the heart, the mouth speaks. You will rarely have to wonder what is in a person's heart as long as you are willing to listen. A person's heart is instantly revealed when he or she begins to speak. People may be trained to hide their intentions for a while, but eventually the words of their mouths will give great clarity to what is truly in their hearts.

We must learn not to think of ourselves first when making a decision in life. For many of us, it is instinctual to first consider how something will affect and impact us before determining how we will respond in a given situation. We tend to do things that benefit us immediately more willingly and seldom get involved when there is no reward or even a delayed gratification.

Followship requires the putting aside of self and what you want or think should be done in a given endeavor. Most people don't want to follow because our desire to give our opinion and have control over things dominates our ability to play a role on a team if we are not in charge. Even the disciples wrestled with their desire to be the greatest and have power. James and John's own mother was guilty of lobbying for her sons' seats in eternity future, wanting them to sit on the left and right of Jesus in the kingdom to come. Jesus told her that authority was not given unto Him to make that decision, but the authority to decide who sits where in eternity belonged to His Father alone.

In order for any team to succeed, all the players have to play the role that they've been assigned.

In theatre or a movie, when reading for a specific role or part, you don't have the luxury of changing the lines or the character to fit what you like or desire. You are required to read what is written and perform what has been asked of you. If you refuse, you will not get the part. You were asked to play a role, and your personal creativity is not needed when desiring to play a role.

Even if you are reading for the lead role, you must submit and follow because the writer or director has a vision for the entire play or movie and you are a piece of the puzzle. Don't forget that in any size puzzle, every piece carries equal value. In a ten thousand piece puzzle, the last piece put in its place is as important as the first two pieces that are connected together. They all are a part of the completed picture. If even one piece is missing at the end of attempting to complete the puzzle, you will look everywhere to find the missing piece, because the puzzle is not complete with even one piece missing.

If you are sent as an ambassador for the US government or are a CEO of a Fortune 500 company and during the negotiation meeting, you decide to speak from your heart and change the course of the meeting based on what you feel or think, you are out of order. Self cannot get involved when you have been sent as a representative of another. True representatives always consider first the heart, attitude, and mission of the one by whom they were sent. Emotions can be dangerous when you are standing in the office as a representative and being given the task of communicating the will of the one who sent you.

On any championship team of any sport, there is a need for the denial of self in order for the team to reach its ultimate goal of victory. For example in football, baseball, basketball, and volleyball, if your agenda supersedes that of the team, winning will usually not take place. Many athletes gravitate to sports that require only one person to compete because some people don't like to put their opportunity to win in the hands of others. Examples of such sports include golf and tennis. Usually, teams that win have the ingredient of great role players, who know their roles and functions, according to the game plan.

Trust is one of the most valuable ingredients in any winning team. Bonds of friendship, even a family connection, are created when a group of people come together with one common goal in mind. The goal is always greater than the individual. You will find your greatest sense of fulfillment when you make happen for others what they have trusted you to pull off for them.

Humility is the answer to selfishness. The Lord has promised that if we would humble ourselves in His sight, that He would exalt us in due season. This due season is literally interpreted as "your" season, which has been ordained and appointed by God Himself from the foundation of the world. Humility is always an opportunity for the individual to initiate. The Lord said to humble "ourselves." You are responsible for your own humility. Humility looks different on every individual. Just because you are quiet doesn't mean you are humble. Some of the most prideful and selfish people in the world are quiet and introverted. The only remedy the Lord has for humility that is not dealt with by the individual is the ministry of humiliation. Life has a way of creating seasons of humiliation, which deal with the root of our pride.

Finally, notice Jesus said to *turn* from your selfish ways. You cannot turn away from someone or something and not turn toward another person or thing. Geography matters and intentional direction is critical. As you turn from your selfish ways, turn to the Lord, for He is the author and the finisher of your faith. Turn toward the one whom you have been called to follow. In doing so, you will have an incredible advantage as you endeavor to walk out the assignment of a life filled with victory and success.

Notes

Chapter 3

Take Up Your Cross Daily

> Then he said to the crowd, "If any of you wants to be my follower, you must turn from your selfish ways, **take up your cross daily**, and follow me."
> Luke 9:23 NLT

Every person on the earth has a God-given purpose and assignment. Throughout the course of your life, you will find yourself in both roles—follower and leader. The cross is your life assignment and purpose. Each person on the earth has a unique and specific assignment. No two individual assignments are exactly alike. Yet, in many cases, our assignments are linked together with others' to help fulfill the purpose for which we were created. Your cross is your life and belongs to you.

Every cross has a responsibility and weight that is custom made for the person's specific capacity to carry. The Holy Spirit is ultimately responsible for revealing to us what our assignment is and what it entails. However, there must be a response and willingness to submit to the plan because the possibility to take our assignment and use it for other purposes does exist. The Lord needs our permission and our participation in order to release and activate His plan for us. Your plan is predestined or preplanned, but you must submit to it for it to be revealed and released. Your entire DNA was intentionally hardwired to prepare you for all the Lord has called you to do and be.

One of the biggest challenges in life as a believer is to remember you are only required to pick up your cross. Actually, you are not graced or anointed to carry another person's cross for him or her. There is a phrase in leadership that Pastor Hart Ramsey uses often, "Stay in your lane." Your lane is your assignment and responsibility. In a relay race, each runner is assigned a lane for a reason. Lane assignments are given for the safety of the runner and other runners in the race, as well as to create the opportunity for each runner to run his or her best race without being impeded by another person. When we cross over into another person's lane in life, we put him or her and ourselves at risk. Many of us have not discovered our own lanes, so it's easy to spend our entire life running in other folks' lanes.

Another ingredient for picking up your cross

is found in the definitive word *daily*. Picking up your cross is not a one-time event that is never to be revisited again. We must daily pick up our cross of purpose and assignment to keep the journey moving forward. That is why so much is mentioned in scripture referring to renewing our minds daily by the washing of the Word of God and dying daily to ourselves. We are tempted on a daily basis to revert back to our own efforts, strengths, and ways that were so familiar to our belief system when the Lord rescued us from our own personal perishing predicament in life.

The man from Cyrene who helped Jesus carry His cross on the Via Dolorosa, while He was on the way to Calvary, gives us the only example in the Bible where carrying another's cross is possible. Sometimes in life, our crosses intersect with others, for the purpose of fulfilling divine destiny. While our cross in life is represented by the vertical taller section of the cross that points to our personal and intimate relationship with our heavenly Father, the horizontal part of our cross will include the relationships the Lord ordains with others who come alongside us to help.

The Lord will always assign provision to true vision. Vision that comes from His heart He is obligated to resource with people, property, and money. The greatest resource in the earth is people. People are God's most precious commodity on the earth, which is proven by His willingness to give His very best in the person of His Son Jesus. God will assign people to your life to help you accomplish what He has put in your heart to do. Every person on the planet is either visionary or missionary in his or her assignment. Visionaries see and cast vision through written and spoken words, while missionaries run with the portion of the vision that has been written and read that they have been trusted to run with.

Every visionary must first be a servant in order to truly be able to relate and be effective. The relationship between leadership and *followship* is critical to accomplishing any vision. You will need help from people to pull off what God has called you to do. We have a confession at Northview Christian Church that says, "God is raising up somebody, somewhere, to use their power, their ability, and their influence to help me." This confession is so important to *followship* because as life plays out, you will have the opportunity not only to be blessed by those the Lord raises up and sends into your world but to be the person that the Lord raises up and uses to bless others as well.

As life continues to move forward, at times, the weight of your cross will seem unbearable. Never forget that Jesus said He would never put more on us than we could bear. His Grace is always sufficient to keep you, no matter what life may present. The only two types of days according to the Word of God are days of prosperity and days of adversity. You never know which day you are beholding. Some days, you will encounter both in the same day. Don't give up, give in, or give out. Jesus is our High Priest, and He has been acquainted with every challenge and temptation we will ever face. He has finished every work for us before the foundation of the world. We must enter into His rest, which is provided through his death, burial, and resurrection.

When we refuse to enter into the Lord's rest, we carry unprocessed burdens or weight that manifests as stress and anxiety. These manifestations are the silent killers of our generation. Many sicknesses and diseases are connected to stress. Our immune system is weakened when we don't handle life's responsibilities properly. The cross we must carry has within it the potential to be heavy.

The enemy has played this card against us for generations. We must learn not only the value of working hard but also the equally important value of playing hard, which includes rest. Jesus told us we could cast all of our cares on Him because He cares for us.

In order to be an effective follower, you must find the balance of life between work and rest. The first revelation of balance is to ask the Holy Spirit to strengthen you with His strength to accomplish what the Lord has assigned for you. You must also know how to recognize when work and rest are necessary. Learning to live in the moment is one of life's greatest challenges for any believer. Most of us live so far ahead in the rat race of life that we forget to enjoy the moments we are currently living in. Life is truly about moments, and every moment has within it the opportunity for an unforgettable experience that makes life worth living. My mother has told me since I left home at eighteen years of age, "Son, don't forget to take time and smell the roses." I didn't know what she meant for about twenty years. I finally understand that she knew something I didn't: life is short! We must learn to enjoy every moment.

In the curse that entered the earth as a result of Adam's sin, the ground was cursed, not work. Work is not a curse; Adam was given a job from the beginning of creation, to tend and care for the garden he was placed in. The ground was cursed with thorns and thistles for the first time. These were enemies to the ground that constantly tried to choke out the production of everything that God had planted. Work is a blessing from the Lord. The Lord promised to bless the work of our hands and to cause everything that our hands touch to prosper. Everything Jacob touched prospered, and everything Joseph put his hands to was successful because the Lord was with him. If your hands are not doing anything, the Lord has nothing to bless and favor.

To truly enjoy your work, you must be connected to something bigger than yourself that you love and are passionate about. One of the ways you know you're doing something you love is when you can do it all day and not keep track of time. Most of the time, work that you love doesn't even feel like work. This can be a blessing and a challenge when you love what you do to the point where you don't take time to rest. Sometimes, a change of scenery is the best medicine. Even still, you will need a plan to recreate and rest in order to have longevity and not allow your cross to crush you and burn you out. Rest and recreation must be intentional in order to make it happen. Financial discipline and stewardship will help you to plan and save money for trips and getaways. Whether you are single or have a family, you will need to take time to rest.

How you handle your cross will determine your ability to be trusted with more. The fast track to promotion and increase in the kingdom of God is to be faithful with little or what you have; you will then be made a ruler over much more. If you are stressed out with what you have, then your heavenly Father will not be able to trust you with more, because He loves you too much to overwhelm you with more than you can handle. The Lord knows our limits, and He knows we are fearfully and wonderfully made. He knows our frames are but dust and that, even at our best, while resilient, we are very fragile.

As a follower, you must master the art of taking what is in your hand and constantly giving it to the Lord so that you will be able to be trusted with more. While casting our cares on the Lord is often advised in churches and pulpits across the world, it is seldom understood and applied to the daily life of the believer. When you cast something, you cannot take it back into your possession. You must relinquish control and all the strings attached to it. It is the ultimate proof of your trust in the Lord. If God is emphatic about anything, it is His desire to be trusted and believed. That is why He tells us to "Trust in the Lord with all our heart and lean not on our own understanding and in all our ways to acknowledge Him and He will direct our paths" (Proverbs 3:5 KJV).

Finally, we must remember that the progression to carry your cross is preceded by your submission to turning from your selfish ways. It's impossible to pick up your cross daily if you have not first turned from your selfish ways. Trying to carry the cross you think is yours is totally different from carrying the cross the Lord has prepared for you. That is why it is critical to first turn from your selfish ways before you take up your cross. Many times, we spend our entire lives chasing our ambitions, not knowing that what the Lord has in store for us is more spectacular than anything we could ever think or even imagine for ourselves.

Trust the Lord to reveal His cross for you. His ways are far greater, better, and more amazing than anything you could ever want for yourself. You were born with His specific intention in mind. Trust the process, even when you can't see the entire picture clearly. The Lord has a way of giving you just enough revelation to start. As you continue to take steps of faith, more will be revealed on the journey. Know this: He will always give you *beginning* grace to start, *continuing* grace to not give up, and *finishing* grace to complete what He has started in you!

The Graces available for every assignment are

1. Beginning Grace.
2. Continuing Grace.
3. Finishing Grace.

Notes

Chapter 4

Follow Who?

Then he said to the crowd, "If any of you wants to be my follower, you must turn from your selfish ways, take up your cross daily, and **follow me**."
Luke 9:23 NLT

Whom you follow is more important than whom you lead. The Lord will always call you to a person before He calls you to a people. In life, we usually concern ourselves with *what* we are called to instead of *whom* we are called to—more specifically, not even whom we are called to, but whom we are called "unto." There is a power in submission that is found nowhere in the kingdom except when you are serving someone.

The progression of *followship* comes to full maturity as you

1. Turn from your selfish ways.
2. Take up your cross.
3. Follow Jesus.

Following is the place where growth and development meet maturity and purpose to forge you into a vessel that is beneficial for the service of King Jesus. Remember—you are not the treasure in earthen vessel, but the treasure is in the earthen vessel and His name is Jesus! Greater is He that is in you than he that is in the world. It is Christ in us who is our eternal hope of glory. In and of ourselves, there is nothing good that we have the ability to produce. We are called to produce fruit, not manufacture fruit. The Lord doesn't want anything we manufacture ourselves. He only wants what is produced through us by the power of the indwelling Holy Spirit. There is no stress in producing, only in manufacturing. True fruit is produced automatically. In and of Himself, everything is good that comes from the life of the Lord Jesus Christ.

Once you discover by revelation *whom* you are called to follow, you will always find whom you are called to lead. Whom you are called to follow is usually an indicator of whom you are being trained to lead. Teachers gravitate to teachers, business leaders are motivated by established business leaders, designers are inspired by other designers, musicians are challenged by other seasoned musicians, pastors are drawn to glean from other pastors, and so on. Don't underestimate the sovereignty of Almighty God and His choosing for your life. Don't think that the person you are called to follow will look like you or even act like you in every area of life. The Lord knows best, and He has already set someone in your path to literally change the course of your destiny for your good and His glory.

> And He goeth up into a mountain, and calleth unto Him whom He would: and they came unto Him. And He **ordained** twelve, that they should **be with Him**, and that He might send them forth to preach, and to have power to heal sicknesses, and to cast out devils. (Mark 3:13–15 KJV)

The first ordination in life is the revelation that we've been ordained to be "with the Lord." Often in business, in ministry, and in life, we go out on our own, instead of waiting to be sent. The sending of the Lord is one of the most powerful and personal dealings that He will ever release upon your life. Everyone wants to go, but few want to sit, learn, serve, and be trained to be sent forth. Hence, the high numbers of failed ministries, businesses, and especially families. We rush into leadership and responsibility without first taking the time to invest in the greatest investment we will ever come into contact with—ourselves.

Sending forth always requires someone else to send you forth. You cannot send yourself and be empowered properly. Impartation always precedes being sent; if you have had nothing imparted into you, what are you taking with you to deliver? That is why Jesus called and anointed His disciples to first be with Him before they ever were sent forth to do ministry. During times of fellowship and exposure in diverse types of interaction, many things are caught as opposed to being taught. Not everything can be learned; experiencing things for yourself creates the most powerful revelations in your life.

When you send yourself, you go on your own power and authority. When you are sent, you go on the power and authority of the one by whom you were sent. Jesus knew this well; it was the core revelation of everything He did on behalf of the Father. When you are sent with delegated authority, you also have the backing of heaven and divine authority because our God is such a fan of order. He does everything decently and in order. With the revelation of the power of being sent, you will walk in greater confidence and boldness to fulfill the assignment you have been given.

Sadly, most people spend more time researching the car they want to buy than researching the person they want to spend the rest of their lives married to. Most of us research business market trends and demographics more than we do the relationships we are so quick to commit to. Relationships are the most important investment in life. Jesus told us that all people would know that we were His disciples based on our love one for another. You must believe in the unfailing love of God for yourself, before you will ever be able to disperse His love to others. Believing the Lord loves you personally releases the strength and power to do anything you have been called to do. The degree to which you have received the love of God for yourself will determine the degree to which you can give His love to others. God is love! He doesn't do love; He *is* love.

Before the twelve disciples were ever a vessel to heal anyone or even preach their first message, they were ordained to be with the Lord. Jesus knew their time with Him was more valuable than anything they could ever do on their own. He was their source of strength and the fuel for their inner fire, which would lead them through many difficult days of trials and tribulations. Even after they were sent out by twos for their first ministry assignment, they came back rejoicing that the devils were subject unto them. Jesus told them not to rejoice because the devils were subject to them but rather to rejoice that their names were written in the

Lamb's book of life. It always has been and always will be about our personal relationship with Jesus.

When you realize the *who* of your following, you only need to find out whom that person is called to serve and you have found your purpose for living. Everybody is called to somebody. If you are sensitive to the leading of the Holy Spirit, you cannot miss the Lord's divine appointment for your life. God connects hearts that are moved by similar things and minds that are alike in spirit.

Elijah and Elisha's relationship is one of the best examples in all of scripture for biblical *followship* and leadership. While Elijah was clear where he was going, Elisha's persistent desire to follow him, no matter what the cost, even to the very end, was evident in the passing of the prophetic mantle from one of the Old Testament's greatest prophets. Elisha asked for a double portion of the anointing and miracles that were manifested in the life of Elijah. By his own admission, Elijah responded that young Elisha had asked a hard thing but nevertheless told him if he saw him when he was taken by the angels, a double portion would come upon him when he picked up his mantle, which would fall. Even as the prophet declared, Elijah was taken by the angels into heaven, his mantle fell to the ground, and Elisha picked it up. The Spirit of God did the rest. It's not a coincidence that Elisha was noted for performing exactly twice as many supernatural miracles as his mentor, Elijah.

Once you know whom you are called to follow, you will eliminate the distraction of multiple voices speaking into your life. Simplify the influential voices that you allow to freely speak into you. Not every one that is talking to you is for you. Not everything that looks right may be right for you. Often, the good is the greatest enemy for those who cannot discern the difference. We live in a dispensation of information overload. Information is literally at our fingertips with Google, social networking, and the availability of Smartphone devices. While this is of great advantage in many ways, it poses a threat to the fundamentals of our society.

For example, the way we communicate has changed drastically within the last ten years. Seldom do people talk face-to-face conversationally anymore. Handwritten letters are obsolete, and most of our conversations are held through e-mail, text, and social networking. Look around the next time you are at a restaurant, office workplace, or even the mall, and you will be shocked by how nonsocial we are becoming. Distractions are in abundance. The need for true fellowship and relationship development impress upon us the importance of these life connections.

Paul instructed the Church to follow him as he follows Christ. This is probably one of the boldest statements made in the New Testament from a believer. He was speaking of imitation, not substitution. He was not saying that he was Jesus, or even perfect like Jesus was and is, but that he was growing in grace and the knowledge of Jesus on a daily basis. His growth was creating a role model for others to emulate. So too should our lives reflect the very life and image of Jesus.

The Greek word *eikon* is our word *icon*, which we use in today's culture. On any computer, you will find on the desktop icons, which hold information that is only opened when you double click on the icon itself. Whatever is inside the folder of the icon, you have access to when you click. In similar fashion, when people click on our lives, they get instant access to whatever is inside of us. Paul was saying, "Be like me, as I am being made like Christ." When people touch your life, do they get you or Jesus? In and of ourselves, we have no power to change, help, deliver, or save anyone. But the Christ in us can do all things through us by His strength.

Being connected to a vision that is bigger than you is critical in learning to follow. In marriage, business, friendships, life, and ministry, the desire to be involved in something that not only is big but that also makes an impact is of top priority to most. It's in our DNA to want to be doing something that has a lasting generational impact. People love helping people instinctively, but the assault the enemy has launched for years challenges this God-given desire, while keeping us focused on ourselves alone. You must daily look past yourself and your desires to fulfill the assignment and role God has ordained for you.

Longevity is achieved more often when there is a common bond to a life assignment that is bigger than you by yourself. We were not sent to the earth to exist alone, doing our own thing, for our own benefit only. Great passion and motivation come when working and serving with others for a common good. Things accomplished alone have little gratification when compared to things accomplished by teams and groups of people. We were created to accomplish things together.

Finally, you must believe that the Lord has your best interest at the center of His heart at all times. He knows all the what, when, where, why, and how of your entire life. Believe that He loves you and that He will never withhold any good thing from you. True *followship* is forged through the private personal relationship you have with the Lord Jesus Himself. Jesus has placed portions of Himself in many people around you in order to get to know Him better. These interactions create insight and revelation you would never get out of any book or class. Life reveals the person of Jesus to us as we interact with those God has connected us to. The Bible explains how "iron sharpens iron" to show us that true sharpness comes when we work together for one common goal and purpose.

Notes

Chapter 5

Jesus Is the Example

Then answered Jesus and said unto them,
Verily, verily, I say unto you, the Son can
do nothing of Himself, but what He seeth
the Father do: for what things soever He
doeth, these also doeth the Son likewise."
John 5:19 KJV

Jesus is the ultimate Divine Follower! The life of Jesus from beginning to end is completely centered on following the example of His Father. His entire purpose and passion was about serving others and not Himself. He proved this during His earthly ministry time and time again. There exists no greater example than His willingness to leave heaven for thirty-three years to testify of the love of the Father toward all humankind. Heaven was bankrupt while the greatest asset of heaven was on assignment to redeem humankind to the Father.

In His first documented encounter after being dedicated on the eighth day, He was found in the temple at twelve years old asking questions of the lawyers and religious leaders of His day. When Joseph and Mary returned to the temple after realizing they had left Him, they asked Jesus what He was doing. His response was, "Did you not know that I would be about my Father's business?" Luke 2:49

His entire life was given as the perfect example of what being a follower looks like. He said throughout His ministry that He was here not to do His own will but the will of the Father who had sent Him. He daily practiced the art of laying down His own will and seeking the will of His Father. The process of *followship* is daily, mostly because our wills are so strong and centered on our personal lust, ambitions, and desires.

In the garden of Gethsemane, Jesus found His greatest challenge as He wrestled with His own will and the sins of the entire world being placed upon Him. After hours in prayer, with the weight and pressure of the sins of the world on Him, causing his sweat to produce drops of blood, He declared, "Not my will, but your will be done." Having been human, like we are, Jesus understands the battle of the will. He was 100 percent God and 100 percent human but knew personally what it feels like to want one thing but ultimately submit to the will of the One who sent you. In order to be a follower,

you must submit to the will of the one who has
sent you.

> I can of mine own self do nothing:
> as I hear, I judge: and my judgment
> is just; because I seek not mine own
> will, but the will of the Father which
> hath sent me. (John 5:30 KJV)

Jesus realized that as a follower, you have the
responsibility of representing the one who sent
you even when it is not convenient or easy. Life
creates fatigue and frustration, but these natural
distractions do not change the assignment you
were sent to fulfill. The most powerful place to live
is in the role of a follower. As a follower, you are
operating in the power and authority of the one
by whom you have been sent. You are not there on
your own authority or power. You are standing in
the role of someone who is greater than you. The
representative does not get to change the script
at the last minute. There is no liberty to take
the assignment and customize it to fit your own
personality. The assignment is not your own.

These truths of *followship* and representation
that Jesus gave us don't just work in the kingdom
of God or church relationships. They work in
every arena of life, business, and relationships.
In corporate America, following is required for
success. In the home, *followship* is required for

peace, unity, and success. In every relationship in life, someone must lead and someone must follow to create the ebb and flow necessary to accomplish the ultimate goal desired.

Sometimes within the same conversation or moment, you will have to lead and follow. That's why it is critical to define every relationship in your life to know who is who, in order to establish the flow of unity.

> How can two walk together unless they agree? (Amos 3:3)

It is always necessary to submit yourselves to one another continuously because our roles and responsibilities can change many times even throughout the course of a week or even in the same day. Being sensitive to the Holy Spirit and respecting the assignments of others around you whom you are connected to will give you greater access to the strengths of the team and ensure success on a consistent basis. You cannot think more highly of yourself than you should because you will miss the insight and revelation that comes in life from the most unexpected people and places. Jesus said, "Out of the mouths of babes, He has ordained praise." You never know who has the answer to your dilemma or circumstance. The Lord can use anyone to get help to you, even angels unaware to minister help and aid to you.

Jesus is at His core a Shepherd. In scripture, Jesus is referred to as the Good Shepherd, Great Shepherd, and the Chief Shepherd. He leads us, guides us, provides for us, protects us, heals us, delivers us, and saves our souls from eternity past unto eternity future by the power of His promise. A young shepherd boy named David knew well the role of a shepherd and the responsibilities His Lord carried as his personal Shepherd. A good shepherd knows the value and protection of following to the health and wholeness of the entire flock. When you try to go off and do your own thing as a sheep or as an individual in life, you put yourself in harm's way.

Jesus knew better than anyone the benefit of leading and following for the betterment of the whole. He was both the ultimate leader and follower in every aspect. To fully understand leadership and *followship*, you need look no further than His life. The arrival of Jesus on the earth is the greatest manifestation of His heart to serve. Even near the end of His earthly ministry, at the Last Supper with His disciples, He was found washing their feet. He was still serving all the way to Calvary's cross. Jesus said that He did not come to be served but to serve. Serving was not something He just did, it was actually who He was. Following the heart of His Father was life to Jesus and where He found His greatest joy on the earth.

Jesus showed us the perfect pattern and secret for successful living through *followship*. His daily pattern of spending private and personal time with His Father revealed His secret weapon of strength. Throughout the life of Jesus, we see a very consistent pattern of Him getting up early, before the disciples, and going to a set place of prayer. During these times of communion and fellowship with His Father, He would worship, intercede, give thanks, and receive instructions for the day. He repeatedly said that He would do nothing without seeing what His Father did first. This implies that each day during this intimate time of exchange, He would see glimpses, in His righteous imagination, of what the Father had already done and what He would be assigned to walk out that day. We see numerous examples of this throughout the Gospel accounts:

> When Jesus lifted up His eyes, and saw a great company come unto Him, He saith unto Philip, Whence shall we buy bread, that these may eat? And this He said to prove him: for He Himself knew what He would do. (John 6:5–6 KJV)

In the miracle of the feeding of the five thousand men, Jesus had been teaching until late in the afternoon and realized it was too late to send the masses home with nothing to eat. He looked at His disciples and told them to feed the people. They knew they didn't have enough money to feed such a mass of people. Interestingly enough, Jesus asked Philip anyway, because He already knew what He was going to do. Jesus had seen this similar supernatural miracle take place in the Old Testament. The account is found in 2 Kings 4:42–44 where many were fed from a small portion. Jesus discovered truth in the Word just like we do today.

Don't presume that He had special power to see or hear from His Father. He saw and heard just like we do to show us the pattern and power a personal relationship with the Lord can produce.

> And as Jesus passed by, He saw a man which was blind from birth. And His disciples asked Him, saying, Master, who did sin, this man, or his parents, that he was born blind? Jesus answered, Neither hath this man sinned, nor his parents: but that the works of God should be made manifest in him. I must work the works of Him that sent me, while it is day: the night cometh, when no man can work. As long as I am in the world, I am the light of the world. When he had thus spoken, He spat on the ground, and made clay of the spittle, and He anointed the eyes of

the blind man with the clay, and said unto him, Go, wash in the pool of Siloam, (which is by interpretation, Sent.) He went his way therefore, and washed, and came seeing. (John 9:1–7 KJV)

When Jesus came into contact with the blind man, He was not caught off guard; he already knew the Father's plan to heal the man for the glory of God to be revealed.

Jesus said, Take ye away the stone. Martha, the sister of him that was dead, saith unto Him, Lord, by this time he stinketh: for he hath been dead four days. Jesus said unto her, Said I not unto thee, that, if thou wouldest believe, thou shouldest see the glory of God? Then they took away the stone from the place where the dead was laid. And Jesus lifted up His eyes, and said, Father, I thank thee that thou hast heard me. And I knew that thou hearest me always: but because of the people which stand by I said it, that they may believe that thou hast sent me. And when He thus had spoken, He cried with a loud voice, Lazarus, come forth. And he that was dead came forth, bound hand and foot with graveclothes: and his face was bound about with a napkin. Jesus saith unto them, Loose him, and let him go. (John 11:39–44 KJV)

When Jesus received word that His friend Lazarus had died, He was not afraid nor was He caught off guard by the report. He already knew what to do because of what He had seen His father do. This may sound strange to believers today, because most of our decisions are made off the cuff or based on our feelings and emotions. But Jesus did nothing without first having seen His Father show Him the way.

True *followship* is seen throughout the Bible. Take a journey throughout the life of Jesus, and you will be amazed at how everything He did was accomplished the same way. Jesus is the ultimate Divine Follower. He is our example for everything that pertains to life and godliness. Follow His lead and trust those He has called you to follow in the earth. Remember—anything He would ever ask you to do in the earth is for your good and for His glory. He loves you and has prepared a way for you that will unlock potential beyond your wildest imagination.

Notes

Chapter 6

Attitude Is Everything

You must have the same **attitude**
that Christ Jesus had.
Philippians 2:5 NLT

Following is more about attitude than gifting and
ability. Many are gifted, but few are available with
the right attitude for service. The earth is filled
with gifted and talented people in every field of
study, business arena, and ministry. However, our
attitude affects the way we see life in general and
controls the way we see every moment of every
day. As a leader, would you rather have someone
on your team with a big gift and bad attitude or a
small gift and the right attitude? I hope you would
choose the latter. A small gift with the right attitude
can always be developed and grow. However, a big
gift with a bad attitude will never grow and cause

you more grief than the thorn in the flesh that the apostle Paul dealt with his entire ministry.

A bad attitude can destroy a friendship, a business, a family, and a ministry, while a good attitude can endlessly bless all of the above. Both a bad attitude and a good attitude are contagious and spread at an amazing rate. People love working with people with a good attitude; people will even change careers just to get away from people with a bad attitude. While you don't choose what type of heart you have, as a believer, you are responsible for guarding your heart and monitoring what you place in it. The Bible warns us to guard our own hearts, for out of our hearts flow the very issues of life.

To study the standard for what your attitude should look like, you must study the life of Jesus. You must not lose the organic, personal, fun, caring nature which He exemplified each and every day. Don't lose the person of Jesus by being enamored with and amazed by the deity of Jesus. While Jesus was 100 percent God, He was also 100 percent human. He even told His disciples in response to their request to see His Father, "If you have seen me, you have seen the Father." Jesus and the Father are one and the same.

Most believers miss the true person of Jesus because the church, for many generations, portrayed an image of Jesus that just was not true. Jesus is not mad or mean or rude or condemning or judgmental. He is kind, compassionate, personable, friendly, patient, and funny. He is someone you want to be around all the time. You must take the time to study the person of Jesus in the Gospel and ask the Holy Spirit to reveal Christ Jesus to you. It is the primary function of the Holy Spirit to reveal Jesus to you.

> But my servant Caleb has a different **attitude** than the others have. He has remained loyal to me, so I will bring him into the land he explored. His descendants will possess their full share of that land.
> (Numbers 14:24 NLT)

Caleb and Joshua were two of the twelve men sent into the Promised Land to spy out the land. While the other ten were afraid of the giants they saw and were overwhelmed by even the fruit in the land of promise, Caleb and Joshua saw things differently. The ten other spies said, "We are not able to take the land that God has promised us." Caleb and Joshua's response was, "We are well able to take the land!" The Lord spoke to Moses, and Moses told all twelve spies that the Lord said He had already given them the land. However, the attitude of Caleb and Joshua affected what they saw. They saw the situation differently than the other ten spies did. The attitude of the ten unbelieving spies caused them to see themselves as grasshoppers in the sight of the giants in the land of promise. Your attitude will always affect how you see yourself and God Himself.

> Since you have heard about Jesus and have learned the truth that comes from Him, throw off your old sinful nature and your former way of life, which is corrupted by lust and deception. Instead, let the Spirit renew your thoughts and **attitudes.** Put on your new nature, created to be like God—truly righteous and holy. (Ephesians 4:21–24 NLT)

As a believer, you have been given a new nature. Your new nature was given to you by the Holy Spirit at salvation. However, the new nature must be put on daily by faith, as a result of the truth learned from Jesus by the inspiration of the Holy Spirit. We were created to be like God in His righteousness and His holiness through believing in the finished work of Jesus and His death, burial, and resurrection. There is no ability to be righteous or holy in and of ourselves. All righteousness and holiness must come by grace through faith in Jesus. The sin of Adam made everything about us unrighteous and unholy. But the life of Jesus has made everything about us righteous and holy.

At salvation, everything that was wrong about us, Jesus took upon Himself for us and everything right about Jesus was imparted unto us, all by faith.

The old you will always try to rear its ugly head and show up at the most inopportune times. That is why the Holy Spirit is daily leading us to renew our minds through the washing with the water of the Word of God. Remember—the old you is rooted and established in selfishness. The root of every bad attitude is selfishness. Attitudes are corrupted when you only look out for yourself in any given situation. When you see someone acting out of character, it is usually that person crying out in a battle of their flesh and Spirit. The flesh is always self-seeking and self-serving, while the Spirit is always seeking to help and serve others. We are continually reminded in the Word to look unto Jesus, because He is the author and the finisher of our faith.

When our attitudes are right, the compassion of Jesus will be the first attribute of His character to manifest in our lives. Compassion is the key ingredient to productivity in the gifts and fruit of the Spirit. Compassion is the foundation for every miracle Jesus performed during His earthly ministry and is the most powerful component of the heart of God as our Father. The fruit of the Spirit is the most accurate portrayal of the person of Jesus. It is critical to know that the gifts of the Spirit are only in operation and power as a result of the presence of the fruit of the Spirit. There are not nine fruits of the Spirit; there is one fruit, and that fruit is love. Love will always manifest Himself in eight different ways, as listed in the book of Galatians:

> But the fruit of the Spirit is **love**, joy, peace, longsuffering, gentleness, goodness, faith, meekness, temperance: against such there is no law. (Galatians 5:22–23 KJV)

In any vessel where the fruit of the Spirit is in manifestation, the gifts of the Holy Spirit will always be accessible and in operation. The gifts of the Spirit without the fruit of the Spirit will always lead to pride and self-promotion. The fruit of the Spirit creates a purity, sincerity, and power that only the Lord can produce. You cannot manufacture the fruit of the Spirit; only the Holy Spirit Himself can produce His fruit in and through you.

When you are tired, guard your heart more because our attitudes can be at their worst when our flesh is weak. Lack of sleep will cause attitudes to manifest in strange ways. Learning the value of rest will keep your attitude and perspective clear. Many times, our judgment becomes clouded when we have not taken the proper and routine times of rest and recreation to realign our thinking. Fatigue keeps your mind from processing life clearly. Many times, the constant barrage of all of life's information will create a feeling of being overwhelmed and overloaded. The way you think affects the way you see. When you are rested, your ability to problem solve is greater. You tend to see more solutions than problems instead of seeing more problems than solutions. Attitude and perspective truly affect everything.

Our daily confessions have a profound effect on our attitudes and dispositions. It would impact your life tremendously simply to say, "I am anointed to solve problems," on a daily basis. Life for a follower and a leader can be reduced to our ability to solve problems quickly and with as little effort as possible. Your ability to solve problems for others is a valuable act of servanthood. People get paid in life based on the value of the problems they solve. In actuality, your life is an answer to someone else's problem. That is why it is so critical not to allow the enemy to rob you of divine connections by having a bad attitude that will hinder the right person seeing you as the answer to a problem.

Life seems to be the most difficult during seasons of testing. Often, our attitudes during these seasons are revealed like never before. Never attempt to vindicate yourself when being attacked. The enemy will use lies, gossip, rumors, and anything he can to cause division, disunity, and discord. He hates unity because in unity, nothing is impossible. Never let insignificant others get in the middle of divine connections. Divine connections must be protected at all cost for the glory of God to be revealed. Refuse to allow others to dictate or determine your attitude toward anything or especially anyone. The enemy's greatest weapon is to use people to create constant drama and chaos in your world. The battle is not against flesh and blood (one another) but against principalities and spiritual wickedness in high places (the devil and his servants). Refuse to fight the wrong enemy, and never fight a battle that has no reward or spoils in being the victor. Many battles have no real reward, so choose your battles wisely and know the one with whom you are engaged in battle. You can't always be fighting.

The solution to our attitude challenge is the art of humility. Humility is the road less traveled, but it is the road filled with the greatest glory and favor. Life is not designed to be hard, but humbling oneself is where life gets extremely difficult for most people. Nobody likes to humble themselves. However, the only alternative to humbling ourselves is to allow life to create situations of humiliation that have a way of forcing us to be humble instead of humbling ourselves. The Lord promised us that if we would humble ourselves under His mighty hand, that He would lift us up in due season. Due season is simply our own personal season and time that He has prepared for us before the world began. No one can hinder, delay, or stop your season, for

God Himself is responsible for ordering your steps and bringing to pass all that He has promised you. Our God is the ultimate Divine promise keeper, who cannot lie and can do anything but fail His children.

You don't always have to be big, but certain moments in life will demand you to be bigger than you really are. In times like these, you must depend on the greater one on the inside of you to stand up while you take the backseat in your own life and follow His lead. The right attitude will take you places in life your gifts and abilities will never take you. The Lord promises us that our gifts will make room for us and bring us before great people in the earth. However, the right attitude is critical to these doors opening and you being allowed to stay, once you have entered. The wisest people in the world will possess an attitude of gratitude.

Notes

Chapter 7

Principle of the Seed

Be not deceived; God is not mocked: for
whatsoever a man soweth, that shall he also reap.
Galatians 6:7 KJV

One of my favorite principles in the Bible is the principle of the seed. We must understand the principle and the power of the seed to unleash the full harvest upon our lives being given in true *followship*. Much error has been spoken throughout generations, dealing with sowing and reaping. The reality is God's only plan to increase our lives is found in the understanding of sowing and reaping. Most of the ignorance surrounding sowing and reaping is found in relegating the principle only to money. This could not be further from the truth.

Actually, money is the least valuable of all of the blessings that come as a result of being a good steward and growing in the area of sowing and reaping. I will use several interchangeable terms in this final chapter to uncover one of life's most misunderstood teachings in the body of Christ. We will talk about the power of a seed, sowing and reaping, and the law of reciprocity.

You may be thinking, *What do sowing seeds and giving have to do with followship?*

In short, your entire life is a seed! Everything you do, say, and even think is a seed that expects to produce a harvest in your life; you are the planter. By and large, we live in a nonagricultural society where planting seeds and harvesting crops are just not something we do often. One hundred years ago, planting was the norm for most families and communities throughout the world. Today, many children have never seen a farm or even crops growing in a field. For some children, the only thing they have ever planted or seen grow is a plant in a science experiment in school.

People, by nature, love to talk about the harvest, but rarely is the value of sowing seeds the topic of our conversations. We also expect a good harvest to come in on time and hope a bad harvest will be delayed to come forth. When we do bad, we pray for mercy, while when others hurt us, we rarely speak of mercy and seem to always want justice. The ground does not care who sowed the seed, only what kind of seed it is. Seeds only produce after their kind. Apple trees don't have to try to produce apples; it's what they do. Orange trees do not need to stress or strain to produce oranges; it's what they do. This is why the apostle Paul told the church in Galatia that God is not to be mocked, because whatever a person sows, he or she shall reap. Even more profound, seeds don't usually just produce one fruit from one seed. A seed has within its DNA the ability to produce a tree with hundreds of fruits. An entire forest can be produced by a handful of seeds.

In the church today, we constantly believe that God Himself, as the Lord of the harvest, is pressing down, shaking together, and running over blessings into our lives. We even confess that God will raise up people to bless our lives in abundance. However, the same must be true for all seeds sown, both good and bad. Unforgiveness is a seed. Bitterness is a seed. Judgment is a seed. Revenge is a seed. These are just a few of the thousands of seeds that are planted daily by unbelievers and believers. Bad seeds produce a great harvest too. As followers, we must be ever mindful of which seeds and how we sow them in our lives to produce the harvest we desire.

> And if you are not faithful with other people's things, why should you be trusted with things of your own? (Luke 16:12 NLT)

When you sow *followship*, you are guaranteed

to reap the same harvest in your future when you are graced to lead. Great followers will always become great leaders. Serving has a built-in reward system, when done with the right heart and motivation. Sowing your life will unlock favor and blessings that you cannot even imagine. Jesus reaped the harvest of abundant life, because He sowed His very life for all mankind as a reflection of the love of His Father. For generations, people have believed that money was life's greatest resource, but in the economy of God, people are life's greatest treasure. Jesus taught His disciples that when you become faithful with money, you will receive the opportunity to have stewardship over God's greatest treasure, people! People mean more to our heavenly Father than anything in His vast creation. Our God, with *Love* as His greatest title, came and died for all mankind. Faithful seeds sown in someone else's field will guarantee your life will be blessed.

> I tell you the truth, unless a kernel of wheat is planted in the soil and dies, it remains alone. But its death will produce many new kernels—a plentiful harvest of new lives.
> (John 12:24 NLT)

The principle of the seed says whatever you put into the ground that dies will resurrect with power and purpose. Jesus said that unless a kernel of wheat goes into the ground and dies, it will produce nothing or remain alone. Only dead things can be resurrected. All believers want to be resurrected, but no one wants to die to him- or herself or for one another. Jesus said that no greater love has anyone than to lay his or her life down for a friend. This is why He laid His life down for the love of the Father to be made manifest. No one took His life. He laid it down willingly as the ultimate Divine follower filled with grace and truth. Every believer desires to know Jesus in the power of His resurrection, but we often fail to read the rest of the verse, where we must know Him in the fellowship of His suffering. Suffering was the seed for the harvest called resurrection in the life of Jesus. If He is our example, then so it is with our lives.

Ironically enough, the world does not have a problem with people being religious. Actually, the world promotes it, unless the name of Jesus is mentioned. You would think the world would desire what Jesus stands for and what He brings to the table, but the opposite is true. The enemy hates Jesus. They are complete opposites in every way. Jesus is Truth, while Satan is the father of lies. Jesus gives life and life more abundantly, while Satan seeks to steal, kill, and destroy. Set your face on our risen King, as the Word declares, looking unto Jesus, the author and the finisher of our faith. As a result, the enemy hates believers too.

Remember—Jesus reminded us that when people persecute us or hate us in this world, it's actually Him that they are persecuting and hating because He is in us. Refuse to be discouraged or afraid! Keep serving and keep sowing for the glory of our great King Jesus!

From our tithes and offerings to our loving one another, sowing is our greatest way to secure a future of prosperity in every area of our lives. The seeds that are sown today are a guarantee from heaven that your tomorrows will be filled with plenty. It is truly more blessed to give than to receive, and this is never seen in greater measure than through the life of a follower. It takes Grace to sow and Grace to receive. Both are necessary ingredients to walk out the promises of God, which in Him, are yes and amen to the glory of God our Father. Life is really about giving the Lord what belongs to Him and receiving from Him everything that has been given to Jesus by ownership. As an heir of God and a joint heir of Christ Jesus, we are to receive by inheritance His finished work.

Following is not weakness; it is actually the wisest decision you will ever make. You don't have to be the lead, or number one, to be valuable in the kingdom. The kingdom of God is filled with number twos, number threes, number fours, number fives, and so on. The clay doesn't get to tell the potter, *Why have you made me this way?* The potter holds exclusive rights to make and use the clay for His own purpose and pleasure. Life is quite contrary. A potter can make a coffee cup to drink from, while some use it for saving coins and others simply collect coffee mugs never to drink out of them. You will never be fulfilled in life until you submit to *who* and *what* the Lord has made you to be.

Reciprocity is a geographical and relational term that simply means that whatever you release will come back to you again. In the natural world, a boomerang would be a great picture of tossing something away from your life only to find it returning again in the same manner. In the kingdom of God, reciprocity is the principle of sowing and reaping. The most exciting part is that Jesus is the Lord of the harvest, and He is ultimately responsible for releasing the harvest into our lives. We must not look to one another for harvest in our lives. The Lord is our reward and the only one from whom true promotion comes. People will disappoint continually, especially when unrealistic expectations are not met or even communicated.

Every person who sows or plants expects a harvest. No one honestly sows a seed just for the fun of sowing. Any good farmer would tell you that sowing is always done with expectation of the harvest to come. As a matter of fact, a farmer would be shocked if he or she had sown seeds and the harvest did not come up. When you sow, sow with expectation, but make sure your expectation is in the Lord, for He cannot fail. Remember—your whole life is a seed from which a great harvest will come so that it will be said of you that you are truly blessed to be a blessing. It would be foolish to expect a harvest in a field you have not sown. Likewise, it is natural to expect a harvest in the fields you have been faithful to sow into.

> Every man according as he purposeth in his heart, so let him give; not grudgingly, or of necessity: for God loveth a cheerful giver.
> (2 Corinthians 9:7 KJV)

Sowing happens as a result of a grateful heart. We are not to give grudgingly or in response to pressure or because we are in need. Our true disposition should be that of cheer, for God loves a cheerful giver. This word *cheerful* literally means hilarious. The reason we are to give hilariously or with great cheer is we know that our future is secured and guaranteed. It's hard not to get excited when you give, especially when you know that our God is the Lord of the harvest and He takes pleasure in the prosperity and wholeness of His children. Jesus told us when a person gives his or her life away, he or she will truly find it, and when a person tries to hold on to his or her own life, he or she will lose it. Remember—giving does not just mean money, but in everything, we give. Our attitudes, personalities, service, talents, forgiveness, and grace are given cheerfully.

I encourage you to give your life away. Ask the Lord today who you are supposed to be following. Someone is praying for you to be a follower. Someone needs your help to fulfill the vision God has given him or her. Your leadership is waiting on your *followship* to mature. The leader you will become is trapped in the follower you have been called to be. Trust the process, for God is forming and shaping something in you that will change the world for good. When you fall, get back up and continue to follow. If you haven't fallen yet, you will. Don't stay discouraged. Keep living, and know this for sure: whatever you do, don't quit!

Keep moving forward. Trust that the Lord knows best. His best is usually hidden in a Divine connection of service and *followship* that will unlock all of heaven's best in your life. Never forget this promise:

> But as it is written, Eye hath not seen, nor ear heard, neither have entered into the heart of man, the things which God hath prepared for them that love Him. But God hath revealed them unto us by His Spirit: for the Spirit searcheth all things, yea, the deep things of God.
> (1 Corinthians 2:9–10 KJV)

Notes

Challenge

My hope and prayer is that this journey on the road called *Followship 101* has been enlightening, edifying, and encouraging to your life. I want to leave you with a challenge that is very unusual and different from any challenge you may have ever received before. Most challenges leave you with a burden or responsibility to do something or try something in order to change your life for the good. This book was not written to be a self-help book. This book was birthed from more than twenty years of experiencing the grace and strength of Jesus through a man who simply believed what Jesus said He could do and that He was who He said He was. Today, I want to challenge you to simply "*be*" who the Lord has called you to be. Rest in the finished work of Jesus Christ and all He has done for you. Believe in the indwelling and almighty power of the Holy Spirit of God Himself, and allow Him to work all things for His glory and your good. Keep your heart open to every divine connection, for God is ordering every step you take. Trust the process!

Grace Blessing

May the love expressed by the Father,
the Grace manifested by Jesus Christ,
and the fellowship created and applied
by the Holy Spirit be upon you!
In Jesus name! Amen!

Printed in the United States
By Bookmasters